# The Art of

# Management

## Practical Advice for Practice Owners

by

## Janice Wheeler

*Illustrated by Esther Moore*

ISBN: 978-1537555515

Published by: The Art Of Management Inc.

THE ART OF MANAGEMENT INC.
200 Ronson Drive, Suite 203
Toronto, ON, M9W 5Z9
Canada

1-800-563-3994

# Table of Contents

## Part 3: Internal Marketing

# Part 4: Time Management

# Part 5: Success

# Forward

Throughout the years, Janice Wheeler, President of The Art Of Management Inc., has written with uncanny insight, about the very real problems practice owners face today.

Under the guise of "quick tips", these pearls of wisdom have been issued to practice owners to help them deal with the situations they face. Many practitioners have kept these weekly articles and are using the information contained in them to bring sanity and focus to the management of their practice.

More than a few have commented that, truly, these have helped them change the way they view and actually manage their practice.

It is our hope that some of these survival tips ring true for you and offer workable solutions that will help you bring success to your practice!

The Team at The Art Of Management Inc.

# PART 1:

# TEAM

# BUILDING

# NUMBER 1

## T.E.A.M.

Definition: "A group of players forming one side in a competitive game or sport."

Very interesting wording: "forming one side". Over the years we have worked with many practices with different quantities of staff, from one doctor and one staff member, up to a practice that had 6 owners and 32 staff. Even in the little ones we have seen the doctor and the staff member on opposite sides, fighting each other's ideas and productivity. In the bigger practices with more players, we have seen cliques that are pitting themselves against each other like they are on opposing teams.

These situations reduce the effectiveness of the staff's efforts, distract everyone from delivering high level care to the patients and clients, and generally lower the pleasantness of working at a meaningful job. Coming into work in the morning can become a chore.

We are all different as individuals and yet have been selected (hired) to be on a certain team called "the office" and like any team, we have to work out how to work together in harmony for the greatest good for the practice and the patients.

One of the reasons we stress making a Mission Statement for the practice is so that there is a common purpose which has been worked out and agreed to by all staff, and it brings everyone together in the accomplishment of that purpose.

T.E.A.M. is an acronym for Together Everyone Accomplishes More. Two people working in concert can accomplish more than two individuals on their own. Three working together achieve more than three working apart. And so on.

Like a hockey team, sometimes the Defenceman will skate down the ice and act like a Forward player in order to accomplish the purpose of the team, i.e. scoring the winning goal. In a good team, the Forward would have quickly assumed the Defenceman's position so there is no chink in the team's armor. Once the goal is scored, they will give back to each other their normal positions. This can also be called Elastic Team Tactics (military term as well as for teams).

If you don't already have a Mission Statement, maybe now would be a good time to create one. If you have one, get it out and dust it off from time to time to make sure all the staff is continuously aligned into a single TEAM.

# NUMBER 2

## Success Through Teamwork

In looking for a great quote to head up this week's help column, we came across so many good quotes from really excellent executives that we decided to just give you a bunch to inspire you and possibly head you in new directions. Look them over and see how you could formulate a higher degree of success in your practice through an increase in teamwork and leadership.

"Teamwork is so important that it is virtually impossible for you to reach the heights of your capabilities or make the money that you want without becoming very good at it."
**– Brian Tracy**

"Talent wins games, but teamwork and intelligence wins championships."
 **– Michael Jordan**

"The greater the loyalty of a group toward the group, the greater is the motivation among the members to achieve the goals of the group, and the greater the probability that the group will achieve its goals."
**– Rensis Likert**

"An empowered organization is one in which individuals have the knowledge, skill, desire, and opportunity to personally succeed in a way that leads to collective organizational success."
**– Stephen Covey**

"The great leaders are like the best conductors – they reach beyond the notes to reach the magic in the players."
**– Blaine Lee**

# NUMBER 3:

## The Winning Team! Perhaps You Have One...

Having worked with many hundreds of Canadian healthcare professionals for 27 years, we've observed that most of them do a fairly decent job of hiring the right staff but they THINK they haven't – simply because they're not coaching them into the winning team.

To help your team achieve DREAM TEAM STATUS, here are 10 suggestions:

1.      Put YOUR practice goals in writing and communicate them to your staff.

2.      Set specific, written POLICY for your practice and have staff read and implement it.

3.      Now you need some written, executable PLANS to achieve those goals, and get the plans being done.

4.      A weekly staff meeting to review stats and set up game plans and targets.

5.      Daily morning conferences help coordinate the various aspects of the practice for the day as a team.

6.      Acknowledge your staff! Thank your team players for being there and doing their jobs effectively.


When and how to correct a staff member is a touchy topic, but keep in mind that all good staff want to know what you want improved. Correct them in private, not in front of others.

Staff incentive plans are an accepted method of acknowledging productivity and, if well designed, will enhance the viability of the practice.

Lead by example. Be positive about how the practice is doing; present the staff with a positive plan of action or get their input on one.

Give your orders clearly and in writing and keep a copy for yourself to follow up on at a specified time.

Of course, there are hundreds of other points to becoming the world's best boss, but start with the above.

# NUMBER 4

## Motivating Staff and The Boss

**Words of Encouragement:**

I was speaking with a staff member of a healthcare practice the other day and she had a problem.

This young woman is the sole staff member in the practice. She told me that her boss never gives her encouragement and wondered what she could do about it. She used to run 12 staff in a company and had been well trained in people skills there. One of the skills she learned was to empower her staff to take full responsibility for their own jobs and to let them know when they did things right and were doing well.

That seems pretty simple and obvious to me as that is what we train our clients to do as executives. However, you may have noticed that staff and bosses come in different sizes and shapes and flavours. Here are some tips to make it easier for both bosses and staff to have a happier team:

**To the Boss:**

In peak production times, things can get quite stressful for you, but also for your staff. A kind word of encouragement or acknowledgement for a job well done will go a long way to creating a happier, more productive team.

**To The Staff:**

Keep in mind that your boss is not only being a boss and running a business; he/she is also the practitioner and therefore has a double stress load and may be feeling a lot pressure. To relieve stress and give support, try to reduce distractions and non-vital questions during the day. And remember, bosses are part of the team too, so feel free to give words of encouragement for a job well done by them whenever you can.

Everyone appreciates being acknowledged for work well done!

# NUMBER 5

## Job Descriptions

Have you ever heard statements such as: "It's not MY job!" "I'm expected to do WHAT?" "How do I do that again?" "I forget what you showed me." "You didn't tell me to do it THAT way." "I didn't know that was part of my job description!"

In all likelihood, these comments are a result of no job descriptions, incomplete job descriptions, or out-of-date job descriptions.

Job descriptions are an essential part of hiring and managing your employees. They should include: the purpose and responsibilities of the job; who do they report to and take orders from; the individual tasks involved with the position; the methods used to complete the various tasks; and so on. Many healthcare positions involve protocols and procedures that need to be learned step by step, often very specific to THAT practice as these can differ from practice to practice.

**Here's a hot tip:**

When you, or one of your staff, are showing a new employee the steps of a procedure or protocol, video the whole thing. I use my big Samsung tablet for this but you can even use your smartphone's video capabilities. Then download these into the computer in a file called job descriptions where the written descriptions for each job are located. Now you have written and videoed job descriptions. These can be referred to until the person has it down cold or re-watched if an error is made. Have fun with this!

# NUMBER 6

## Spelling It Out

### Job Descriptions and a Policy Manual:

If one doesn't know where the goals posts are in a soccer game, and one doesn't know that it's their job to kick the ball in there to win the game, one probably won't remain long on that team. A play book, a coach and lots of training will often straighten that team member out and turn them into a spectacular player.

Similarly, practices need to have a play book [policy manual and job descriptions], a coach [the owner and/or office manager], and lots of training. The result will be a spectacular team delivering the highest quality service and care to the patients or clients of the practice.

### Policy Manual:

A policy manual must contain:

1.      The goals to be achieved by the practice

2.      The rules of the game [such as how and when you can take holidays, what to do if you wake up too sick to come to work in the morning, what to do if you notice some supplies are low, etc.]

3.      The protocols and systems for the office

4.      Job descriptions for each position in the practice

5.      And so on.

When a new employee joins the practice, they must be required to read the entire policy manual to learn the specifics of how their new team operates.

## Job Description:

A job description is defined as a detailed written account, agreed between management and staff member, of all the duties and responsibilities which together make up a particular job. These lay out the specifics of a position within the practice, the job title, who the post holder reports to, what the purpose of that position is, how it relates to the other jobs within the practice, and lists out the exact duties, responsibilities or functions that must be carried out by the post holder.

## Service:

As part of the policy of the practice, any staff member is expected to take responsibility for the overall success of the practice. Team work is very important and SERVICE is the number one concern overriding any "rules" or "policy" to the contrary. For instance, a patient or client walks in the front door and the receptionist is not present. Another team member notices this happening and steps up to the plate to take care of the client. This policy prevents the "it's not my job" syndrome.

A team that is fully trained, running on agreed upon policy, and has service as their overriding purpose will help generate a full and busy practice.

# NUMBER 7

## The Ideal Employee

If one were to stand in the shoes of an employer and ask oneself, what are the qualities of an ideal staff member, one might find the following items are on the list:

1. Don't be a clock watcher. If you come early each day and stay till your job is done, even if it means being a bit late, this lets your employer know that you care about your job and the practice, and you will make a positive impression.

2. Take pride in how you dress and groom yourself. Appearances are very important in a practice as patients will assess your competence by their initial reaction to your appearance. Sloppy clothes and hair and no make up reveals that you may not have an eye for detail and perhaps lack professionalism.

3. Keep upbeat and friendly. Be known as the person who always has a positive attitude. It'll make for a better work environment for the other staff and yourself.

4. Go for being top notch at what you do. Strive for excellence in your work.

5. Do not bring personal problems into the office. Neither the other staff nor patients should know about any problems you are experiencing in your personal life. Anything that brings the other staff "down" is destructive of the practice.

6. Never text or email personal communications during business hours. Your employer is paying for you to give patients perfect service and to help him or her to grow the practice. There is never a shortage of work to do.

7. Ditch the clutter. Keeping your area of the practice neat and uncluttered will make it easier for you to produce, as well as looking good to the patients.

8. Don't fall apart under pressure. Take a deep breath, calm yourself, and look objectively at what needs to be done, first step then next step and get started. Collapsing under pressure reveals weakness, not strength.

9. Facebook and social media require intelligent use. It has become a cause for dismissal if one bashes their employer or practice on social media and reveals a lack of professionalism. Keep those rants private.

The fact is that having and exhibiting as many of these qualities as possible will have a direct influence on the success of the practice. You will earn respect at the same time.

# NUMBER 8

## I thought we discussed this ...?

Practice owner: "I distinctly remember giving you the order two weeks ago to order those supplies."
Staff member: "No, you didn't, I would remember if you had and I would have done it."
"Yes, I did tell you to do it." "No, you didn't! Don't blame it on me."

Fighting words that cannot be taken back, and neither side wins that argument.

Why? What's wrong with this picture? You delegated like you are supposed to, didn't you?

Ever heard the famous saying, "If it isn't written, it isn't true?" This is one of those moments when the saying couldn't be truer. Efficiency experts know that a lot of time can be wasted waiting for verbal orders to be complied to, only to find that they were never carried out, sometimes resulting in a disaster.

*Here is a very simple time-saving system that can help you prevent this massive waste of production time.*

1. When you give an order, do it in writing, be very specific, ask for a reply and give a date for it to be done by. For example, "Please call our software company and ask them to quote on the latest upgrade and send this order back to me with a note to let me know that it was done and what happened. Please have this done by 4 days from now."

2. The order can be handwritten or done on the computer but you must make a copy of it.

3. Give the original to the staff member.

4. Keep the copy in an "Orders Pending" file folder on your desk. When you get the compliance report back, you can match it with the copy you kept and destroy both, if the order was satisfactorily completed.

5. Once a week, on your Executive Time (hint, you are supposed to have a period of time each week that is devoted to management of the practice) you should go through this file as a habit and see if there are any uncompleted orders lurking still. If there is one (or more), follow up with the staff member to find out what is happening. Work out a solution to getting it done and put a fresh date. Put the order back in the file noting the new date that it is to be done by.

7. If you still don't get compliance, there are a few things that could be wrong and you should check for these:

**(a)** Does the staff member concerned have a job description and does it clearly state the purpose of her job? Does she understand this purpose? Does she see that the order you gave falls within her job description (if it does – if not, this is your "bad" and you should give it to the person who it DOES belong to as an order)?

**(b)** Ask her or him what's happening with the order. Clear up anything not understood about it.

**(c)** Did the person need training to carry out the order, and if so, did they get it?

You sometimes have to be very patient and you may find it hard not to just do it yourself, but if you do, you have failed the boss and persistence tests. Given that you have hired the right staff member in the first place, then it is a matter of pushing through and getting your orders complied to and it will all come out alright!

# NUMBER 9

## Not All Rowing in the Same Direction?

Do you sometimes feel that you're not all pulling in the same direction? Ultimately, the whole team is supposed to be there to give every patient or client who walks in the door the 5 Star Care they are paying for. Somehow that generalized purpose "sounds" great, but in the day to day world of the practice, not everyone keeps their eyes on that horizon or even knows exactly what that means.

You may feel that you have the correct individual team members and that they are each stars in their own right, but yet they are not all pulling together in the same direction.

On the other side of the equation, not all bosses have charted the path to his or her horizon. If you're trying to steer the ship in a certain direction, it's nice for the staff to know what that is.

**Mission Statement:**

As the owner of a healthcare practice, one of your first duties is to work out the Mission Statement for your practice. It should be fairly comprehensive and upbeat with believable goals that can really be achieved. Then you can issue positive directions on a weekly basis that align with the Mission Statement. That way all concerned are focused on reaching the same goals.

A Mission Statement is not just something you stick on the wall and admire, but rather it is something all in the practice should live and breathe. Get your staff's input on it too if you like. It can be broad in scope or very specific.

Remember: You can't get there if you if you don't know where THERE is.

# NUMBER 10

## How to Destroy a Really Great Staff Member

You can hire the best of candidates to join your staff team – she has the right experience and good enthusiasm and lots of good ideas. She also, from her side of the picture, has high hopes that YOU are going to be a great leader and that you know how to train her so she can quickly gain control of her duties, and that you will allow her to demonstrate her competence. She starts with the anticipation that she is going to do a super job for you.

However, somewhere along the line this picture starts to erode. You notice her mistakes and correct her, you don't give her enough validation and compliments to overcome the number of corrections; she also notices that you don't trust her yet because you double check her on everything. Or, in the alternative, she may feel that you have a lack of interest in what she has accomplished or is getting done because you don't communicate with her much at all nor give her directions and goals to achieve.

Additionally, she may have observed that you are quite overloaded and she offered to take on additional tasks such as doing the ordering of supplies or doing the bookkeeping or planning some promotion or marketing, but you put her off saying you like to do those yourself and that it would take too much time to train her. She then gets frustrated because you won't delegate more to her so she can really help you. Great staff like to accomplish a lot and get things done.

In a nutshell, how to ruin a really great staff member is to fail to be a good leader and to delegate more to her so she is challenged in a fun and fulfilling way. Instead, you send her spiraling down from enthusiasm into boredom or lower because she isn't allowed to contribute fully and is not allowed to demonstrate her competence. Most staff are not lazy – just under-appreciated and under-utilized.

Good leaders do not train followers, they train leaders under them. Delegate more and have great, happy staff.

# NUMBER 11

## Monkeying Around

Going in to work every day can be a drudgery or a feel like a duty to show up. Same old, same old. Everyone reports in and gets on with the day.

Then there are the bad news bears (sometimes patients, sometimes staff) that bring in negativity and bad news to the practice. Brings everyone "down" and rains on the day.

But where's the fun? Where's the razz-ma-tazz? Going to work and giving great care and service to the patients is supposed to be uplifting and interesting.
Have you ever noticed how much gets done in a day where everyone is "in a great mood," and that on those days, things run smoothly?

**Put the fun back into the practice:**

Well, here is a tip on how to bring the tone of the group up a few notches and create those "special" days everyday. I got this idea from a friend who said it turned around his whole team.

It has to do with a certain stuffed monkey (a really cute one). It is an award and is given at the weekly staff meeting to the staff member who did the most to bring the other members of the team "up" that week. All the staff got into it and the whole mood of the office lifted from the minute they started it.

**Increase team cooperation and morale:**

The team cooperation improved, the number of "problems" dropped, their clients noticed the change and production skyrocketed with the morale increase.

The cute monkey became a coveted award and everyone worked hard to earn it. Try this idea on for size and see what happens! Should be as much fun as a barrel of monkeys!

# PART TWO:
# LEADERSHIP

# NUMBER 12

## Practice Management – A Leader Is Created

If you are not a "born leader," take heart. Most real true leaders are created in the crucible of life, or else by mentoring, or by actual training.

However we get there, we all need to be leaders in our own endeavors if we are to be successful.

Whether you own a practice with no staff or with many, you still need to bring certain qualities and skills out in yourself in order to achieve your goals.

A leader, a boss, a coach, a manager, an executive.

Do these titles all add up to the same thing? In short, pretty much yes. Here are definitions for each of these titles that shed some light on some of the skills you need:

1.   **Leader:** a person who leads; directing, commanding, or guiding head, as of a group or activity

2.   **Boss:** a person in authority over employees, as an employer, a manager, or a foreman

3.   **Coach:** an instructor or trainer; the person who is in overall charge of a team and the strategy in games

4.   **Manager:** one who manages a business, etc.; one who manages affairs or expenditures, etc.

5.   **Executive:** one who holds a position of administrative or managerial responsibility in an organization

**A ship tossed to and fro:**

Most healthcare professionals have taken a number of courses over

[36]

the years, but they usually were not about how to manage a professional office. A client once told me: "The result is that with time, a practice with no skilled leader or management plan becomes like a ship without a rudder and is unable to steer in any set direction. The practice can become like a ship tossed to and fro with every wave that comes its way. Becoming a good leader is necessary in order to put your practice on an even keel and set a true course."

As the owner of a business that was started from scratch, it all starts with you and your goals for the future. Some folks have bought an existing practice or inherited one, and in which case you have to slowly change aspects of the existing practice to meet your own vision for it.

Many practice owners are under the common misconception that if they have no staff or only one or two, they don't need to bother to learn how to be a good boss or manager. However, the reverse is actually true because without these skills, you will remain a one-man band, single-handing everything, overworked and underpaid.

Here are tips that you can start applying right away.

**Your role as a leader:**

Here are a few quotes from famous leaders which highlight some good leadership qualities:

**1. You are the Goal Setter:**

"The first responsibility of a leader is to define reality. The last is to say thank you."
- Max DePree

**2. You are the Director:**

"Leadership is the art of getting someone else to do something you want done because he wants to do it."
- Dwight Eisenhower

### 3. You are the Courageous One:

"Courage is being scared to death, but saddling up anyway."
- John Wayne

### 4. You Produce Leaders:

"I start with the premise that the function of leadership is to produce more leaders, not more followers."
- Ralph Nader

### 5. You are the Spark that Causes Change:

"Cause change and lead. Accept change and survive. Resist change and die."
- Ray Norda

Challenge yourself to expand your leadership qualities and skills. You can even take one quality per week and make it your focus. If you have staff, get them to do the same and make it a game. At the end of the week, have a short meeting and discuss how it went and how to improve further.

# NUMBER 13

## Practice Not Going Anywhere Fast?

Over the last 27 years, I have spent at least 3 – 4 hours with over 6,000 healthcare professionals analyzing their practices one-on-one, and I have found many, many reasons why a practice may not be going anywhere fast.

Here are the first things to consider:

1.      As the practice owner, do you have a clear vision of what you would like your practice to be in an ideal world? Aspects to consider: production targets, aesthetics of office, team size and training, ideal type of patient or client, location (rent or own), and so on.

2.      Have you put these goals in writing?

3.      Do the staff of the practice know what these are?

4.      Are the staff in agreement with these goals?

5.      Have you worked out a strategy of how to change the existing set of circumstances towards meeting your ideal scene?

6.      Have you issued this strategy or the steps thereof to your team to help get them done?

These are the top level considerations and decisions that MUST be made before you correct or change anything else. Take some time to sit down and work this through.

Remember, you can't "get there" if you don't know where "there" is.

# NUMBER 14

## The 4 Stages of a Practice: From Love to Hate

Just as products have a life cycle or shelf life, so do practice owners and managers. You can go from the fun stage (when you first started up) to the final stage of "I hate my practice and I want out" (which can go on for many years).

The question is: Can something be done to break this cycle and go back to the FUN stage? The answer is YES! Here's how it goes …

### Stage 1:

This is the Vision-Maker Stage. When you first started or bought your practice, you were having FUN, creating and envisioning a very bright future. You probably didn't even blink about working 24/7 on getting it going. It was your baby. You were being the CREATOR. You had a thousand ideas and were totally into getting them accomplished.

### Stage 2:

This is the organization stage. You now need staff and to organize for expansion. You have become the Manager and your attention is on handling present time and you tend to stop progressively creating the future.

### Stage 3:

This is the coping stage. Forget the creating and envisioning bit. You're not even a manager any more, but more of a problem solver (or babysitter). You are not having so much FUN. You are coping with undone actions stacking up and the feeling of drowning or overwhelm. Life is rushing by you.

## Stage 4:

You are now in the HATE Stage! You start thinking of selling (though it is a bad time to do it because the stats have usually gone down by this stage and your practice will sell for less). You are definitely no longer having FUN.

### Your Vision for Your Future

You need to get back in the VISION-MAKER mode, Stage One. Ideally, you could steal one hour per day out of your schedule (or a couple of hours per week) which is inviolate in order to PLAN the future. This is your number one priority: CREATE THE FUTURE. Put a lot of attention on it. Do research on other people's website (this is called market intelligence … or spying) to see what they are doing, what is their competitive advantage, what cool things are they doing for their patients and their staff.

### Inspire Your Staff

You need also to pass on this VISION to your staff. INSPIRE them. Constantly. Start off each day with good news and compliments and a reminder of why your practice is there, i.e. the VISION. Go over ideas for the future with your staff at the weekly staff meeting. Get input from them. Another idea: What socially responsible activities can you be involved in as a team (raising money or contributing time and effort to some worthy cause). And so on.

### Executive Time

Start by working out a cast-in-concrete time to do your future planning each week. If you don't MAKE that time, you will stay in Stage 3 or 4 forever.

In my company, I did come in one hour early each day this week and we have a new company vision: "Changing the way the world manages." And we worked out as a team what our product is: "Inspired and highly successful clients who have now achieved the freedom to work and live their lives the way they always wanted to."

What is your VISION? What inspires you? Let us know what you come up with. We love feedback.

# NUMBER 15

## Your Role as A Leader

As the owner of a healthcare practice, you wear a dizzying number of "hats" (functions) and sometimes you may feel a bit bounced around and stressed by the end of your workday.

Your main duties as the CEO of your practice (besides being the healthcare provider) are: leader, boss, coach, manager and executive.

Here are some dictionary definitions:

**Leader:**

• a person who leads; directing, commanding or guiding head, as of a group or activity.

**Boss:**

• a person in authority over employees, as an employer, a manager, or a foreman.

**Coach:**

• an instructor or trainer; the person who is in overall charge of a team and the strategy in games.

**Manager:**

• one who manages a business, etc.; one who manages affairs or expenditures, etc.

**Executive:**

• One who holds a position of administrative or managerial responsibility in an organization.

**To sum it up:**

1.    You are the goal setter.

2.     You are the director.

3.     You are the analyzer.

4.     You produce leaders.

5.     You have courage.

6.     You are persuasive.

7.     You follow through on actions.

8.     You think in new combinations.

9.     You never doubt you will succeed.

10.    You know what you want and go after it.

11.    You focus on your future success.

12.    You are frank, forthright and honest.

13.    You can change your mind.

14.    You believe things will turn out well.

15.    You always strive to do better.

16.    You think about others' needs.

17.    You are patient with others.

# NUMBER 16

## Intention Wins Every Time

**Some wonder if there is a "secret formula" for building a great practice. Well, there IS a basic, or underlying, formula.**

It is a very short formula, one word: **INTENTION.**

Let's take a look at exactly what intention is. According to Webster's New World Dictionary, intention is the "determination to do a specific thing or act in a specified manner". Also, "aim, end, or purpose." As the executive of the practice, you have goals that you want to achieve with the practice (if you don't, you should!). You also give directions or orders to your staff to accomplish certain steps that you set up toward the attainment of the goals.

Once you have formulated your goals, you then need the *intention* (determination) to get them met. It's the one element that, if not present, your chances of success in any venture are next to nothing. We 'intend' things all day long. We intend to get up in the morning and we do. We intend to go to work and we do. The difference here is that getting up and going to work don't require THAT much intention simply because they are short-term actions. Actions that are longer term, such as building your practice, require *sustained* intention. In other words, **PERSISTENCE**. That is, you don't just intend it once and then give up, hoping that it will all work out. Your intention needs to be there all the time, non-stop — persistent.

As an example, in your marketing efforts, you would first formulate your intention, i.e. what do you want to achieve? Once you get the marketing plan in place and running, you must then maintain the *consistency*; don't let up or slack off. Another point to consider is that if you **INTEND** to get something done, **PERSIST** until it is. The biggest faux pas we see in practices from the executive end is not pushing through until you have achieved your aim.

If you are not putting all of your intention into building your practice, and things haven't been going well, then you'll continue to have things 'not going well' unless you change something. Intention is what wins the game, every time. If you need help in your practice, don't hesitate to get it. The longer you wait, the longer you will suffer with bad conditions and problems.

It takes courage to have intention and carry through. It takes courage to not give up. Intention also carries with it the responsibility of doing what you intend to do. So take full responsibility for your own decision to be successful and DO what needs to be done in order to succeed and you'll see – intention wins every time.

# NUMBER 17

## Force vs. Intelligence

To succeed, you need both force AND intelligence. If you use the correct amount of each, at the right times, you will succeed at anything you do.

**Unsuccessful Leadership:**

You can find unsuccessful management everywhere. Certain leaders are too forceful: "Get 5 New Patients scheduled by tomorrow or you're fired." They might have short-term success, but never long-term success.

Other unsuccessful leaders are the intelligent "nice guys." They say, "By increasing the number of New Patients up over last year, research shows that the Collections will also be higher than the year before."

**The Winning Combination:**

To succeed in your battle for success, you need your own balance of force and intelligence.

A successful executive not only does good planning (intelligence) and gives precise instructions, he or she must also have enough persistence and intensity (force) to push the plans through.

For example, the boss concludes that the fees are too low. He writes an order raising the fees. The staff objects. The boss maintains a position and insists on the price increase despite all opposition. To succeed, and have enough money to pay the staff, the boss must not waiver.

Successful business owners not only work out policy and guidelines for the staff, they enforce those policies. No policies and no enforcement are both unsatisfactory.

You can spend all day planning your success, but you also need to work as many hours as necessary to make it happen.

If you are not being as successful as you would like to be, which do you need to increase: intelligence or force, or maybe both?

# NUMBER 18

## Leadership Qualities

Whether you know it or even want it as a title, everyone is a leader in some part of their lives. Mothers and fathers are leaders. Owners of practices are leaders. Staff can be great leaders within the practice as well.

Great leaders have many defining qualities and some of them are listed below. What ones are you good at and which could use some work:

- **Knows where he/she wants to get to**
- **Confidence in his/her goals**
- **Good communication skills**
- **Even better listening skills**
- **Ability to see the positive qualities in another**
- **Skill in coordinating teams and schedules**
- **Respect for their staff**
- **Courage to make decisions**
- **Persistence in follow through to get the end result**
- **Self-motivated - can admit when wrong**
- **Trusting of others and themselves**
- **Being available to the team**

Getting most of these going in yourself will give you the power to be a good and strong leader. Practice one each week and enjoy the results.

# NUMBER 19

## 4 Great Leadership Skills Anyone Can Apply

In the current marketplace in Canada, there is a growing sense of change and uncertainty. Therefore, as the owner or manager of a practice, more skill is required than ever before to maintain an even keel and efficient course to optimum productivity from yourself and your team players. You must give them a sense of security while pushing them to achieve greater heights.

How can you do this? Simpler than you think! Here are just 4 ways to start with:

**1. Be caring and interested in each member of your team.**

I put this one first because you don't want to ever lose sight of that ability. Your staff can sense whether you actually care about them or not. They are there to help you achieve the goals of your practice. Treating them like cogs in a wheel will not elicit top performance from them. Anyone will shine more brightly and work harder if properly cared about.

**2. Have a strong business plan and make it known.**

There is a famous saying: "You can't get there if you don't know where there is." Your team has chosen to work for you, but they need to know where the practice is headed and what you expect of them in the actualizing of those goals. Clear direction and a passion for your service can galvanize the team into high levels of productivity.

**3. Project Positivity.**

Remember the game "Follow the Leader?" In a practice, good employees look to the leader to set the pace of how work is going to be done. If you exude positiveness when giving direction or asking for production, the staff will feel a confidence and control factor that they in turn will project into their work. Further, acknowledge good production and efforts. Be positive about advances the practice is making. Do not dwell on negative aspects with your team.

### 4. Issue clear and concise orders.

As a boss, it is uber important to be very clear and concise and firm in the directions you are giving your staff. Tossing off an order to "finish that project quickly" does not always lead to immediate compliance. Instead, give an order such as "I need that report on my desk by 5 p.m. today so that I can read it over tonight and be prepared for my presentation tomorrow morning at 7 a.m. If you have any questions, please ask me." This is very precise and gives the staff a timeline and a reason for it that they can then think with and comply to.

Have fun embracing these skills and remember to enjoy the fruits of your own labour as a **GREAT** leader!

# NUMBER 20

## Are you an Inspiring Leader?

Sometimes life can feel a little flat and not so interesting and you may wonder why you even bother doing what you do. Especially after a patient or client dumps all over you for something you did or didn't do. And to make matters worse, if you are the boss, you are supposed to be inspiring your staff to be better, more brilliant, more productive, total geniuses at dealing with your patients.

How do you pull yourself up by your own bootstraps and get your own self-motivated first? Hah, there may just be an answer...

**Inspiring yourself first:**

Here is a simple technique I use with myself and it works for me. I get inspired and feel happier. Give it a try and see if it works for you too.

You need a quiet space where no one will bother you for a few minutes. You can have a pen and paper handy if you would like to write down some notes because you will want to pass on to your staff what you think of.

Okay, here is what to think of: Recall each patient or client you have dealt with that you made happier in some way, made smile, changed their life for the better, did something amazing for them, pulled off a miracle treatment, etc. Keep focused only on the positives. Write their names down so you remember them when going over these in a staff meeting.

If you do this exercise correctly, you will feel like a million bucks again and very proud of what you do and will feel like doing more of it.

Then pass this inspiration on to your team and get them inspired too!

**This is the end result of working with each of our clients:**

"Inspired and highly successful clients who have now achieved the freedom to work and live the life they have always wanted to."

# PART 3:

# INTERNAL MARKETING

# NUMBER 21

## Is Marketing Driving You Crazy?

Marketing, marketing, marketing. Once upon a time, you just had to rent a space (oops, marketing), put a sign out front so people knew you were there (oops, more marketing), and you would attract patients or clients who would then tell others about you (oops, even more marketing), and your practice would fill up.

Hmmm…. It's always been about marketing then, hasn't it? However, times and methods and quantity of marketing required to compete for the public's business has evolved and so you need to be at the head of the class in this subject in order to have a top practice.

**What is marketing? It is making yourself and your practice known to potential patients or clients and giving them a reason to choose you over other options available to them.**

And there are endless ways to do so. With the internet, the whole world can see you if you are present there. However, don't leave out the myriad of other ways to market.

**Some standout rules of marketing:**

**First rule**

Almost any marketing method is better than no marketing at all. However, there are things that work much better than others and will make the public think **WELL** of you and **WANT** you as their healthcare provider.

**Second rule**

Decide on your target market. What kind of patients or clients do you want to attract? If kids are not it, don't have pictures of kids in your messages. If seniors are it, then have pictures of seniors. (For vets, most of you do this very well with logos or pictures that show what animals you treat.)

## Third rule

Look different – you're competing for attention. Receiving a shiny postcard in the mailbox at home has become quite a common sight. But they all look the same and say the same thing. What if you did something a little different? Watch for promo pieces you receive in your mailbox that catch your eye and compel you to read them to see what it's about. Save these in a file and next time you get a flier designed, show your designer what you like best about each piece so he or she can combine the ideas into a piece that is uniquely yours. The same applies to websites, Facebook pages, Twitter, LinkedIn, Pinterest, and so on. Surf the web frequently to look at other providers' sites. There are blow-away websites there that will inspire you. Keep a list of these and show your web designer what you particularly like in each one.

## Fourth rule

Say something different. Ask and talk about the prospect's needs. A list of services that your practice offers is boring and does not impinge on the reader. Asking questions about the prospect's health or issues will engage them by making them think in the direction you want them to.

## Fifth rule

Don't waste your marketing efforts. Almost every marketing action you take drives the potential patient or client to your Receptionist with questions, which, if properly handled, will result in a new patient. (These calls are not from people who are sitting at home dialing healthcare practices because they have nothing better to do. They have a need.) While some Receptionists are highly expert at converting this "reach" into your practice into a new patient or client, most have little to no training in how to handle "shoppers" (but try their best). Most practices lose 2 – 5 potential new patients per week because of this point. Sales training for them is essential if you don't want to waste your marketing dollars and time. (AMI's Sales Workshop spends some time helping them learn this skill.)

So there you go – use these rules well and fill up your practice with patients you love to treat!

# NUMBER 22

## Who's in Charge of Marketing?

With each healthcare professional I meet one-on-one for the free practice analysis we offer, one of the many questions I always ask is: **"Who's in charge of your marketing?"**

Over the last 25 years, I have gotten quite a variety of answers:

- What marketing?
- Nobody!
- We don't do marketing in our practice – all our new patients are from word of mouth (that's because they don't do any other marketing).
- Me?

The next question I ask is: **"Do you have a written, organized Marketing Plan?"** The answer has been resoundingly "no." The next question is: "Is it because you don't think one is necessary or is it because you don't know how to do one?" The answer is usually the latter.

The point is: If you want a lot of new patients coming in the front door, you need to market (in addition to increasing the word of mouth by your patients, of course). **You have to make yourself known and chosen by all the right people.** This is called Target Marketing.

Don't subscribe to the theory that "if you build it, they will come." That is passive marketing and it is a slowwww way of growing (at best). Pro-active marketing is the way to go, whether by fliers, open houses, fun events, give-aways, sponsoring teams, social media marketing, websites and other Google marketing methods, YouTube videos, podcasts, email newsletters once a month to your patients, etc. etc. etc.

**There is absolutely no shortage of cheap and easy marketing methods.** The main thing is to decide who is in charge of your marketing and then get a written marketing plan in place and **START**. If your marketing is not driving the New Patient numbers up, change it up and try again. **Don't relax on this.**

# NUMBER 23

## Low Cost or No Cost Marketing

Want more new patients but don't want to spend a fortune on marketing? Why should you when there is so many brilliant, free and easy ways to go about it?

Our team spent 1-1/2 hours one morning last week putting our heads together to come up with a list of inside out marketing ideas for ourselves and for you … there are many, many free or low cost internal marketing methods that can be done from within the practice. We filled 1-1/3 typewritten pages with ideas and then farmed out the first few ideas to specific individuals according to their interest and/or skill set and there is one person delegated to follow up that each thing gets done.

Here are a few of the ideas, and you can probably use some of them in your own practice as well. These are not in any order of priority or significance:

- Learn how to do posts on Twitter and set up a Twitter account and get going – one staff member will maintain this and the rule is to keep them short and business related and positive.

- Have different staff do short podcasts on various topics to do with your practice and put them on website, Facebook, etc.

- Have staff do a testimonial of why it is rewarding working in your practice and post on Facebook, website, Twitter, and so on.

- Make a Google Plus page on your website and each week ask a few of your patients or clients to post on it why they like your service and practice.

- Have a "Company Press" blog on your website with the latest news about the practice or the staff (i.e. who's pregnant, getting married, got a new puppy (picture please), went on an interesting trip (pictures please) etc. Makes patients feel included in your business.

- Make an introductory video for your practice – put on Facebook, website, LinkedIn etc. Staff can do it and feature the doctor in one part.

- Make a FAQ (Frequently Asked Questions) page for your website.

- Make a bunch of YouTube videos about topics that patients want to know about your type of service

- Have a Q & A page on your Facebook

- Write short articles (in layman language) and get them posted on various blog sites, Facebook, website, etc.

- Ask patients/clients to link with you on LinkedIn.

Those ideas are just to name a few!!! You can probably come up with many more if you and your team put your heads together.

The main trick is to not overwhelm yourselves with too many ideas. Just take a couple and **GET THEM DONE**. Have someone in charge of the completion of the targets and dates set by which each one will be done. Most of them are fairly quick to set up. Then they just need to be maintained.

Once the first couple are done or in "maintain mode", take the next few ideas and get going on those.

Remember: **You can make tomorrow even better than today!**

# NUMBER 24

## Image, Image, Image

Want to have more new patients walking in your front door? Maybe you need to improve your front door! One of the easiest ways to increase new patient numbers is to update the image your practice projects.

Many practices, having been around for a while, get a sort of tired, unchanging look that patients actually subconsciously notice. Referrals by your existing patients can subtly suffer as a result.

There are many inexpensive ways to improve the look of your practice and you should continually look for ways to change it up and impress your patients.

**See for yourself:**

Take a drive and look at the front of other healthcare professional's practices, storefronts and other businesses, and note down what it is you like most or least about each one.

Now go across the street from your practice and look at it as if you were a new patient or someone just considering using your services. Does it look upscale and inviting, or is it dull and ordinary? Is your sign visible, eye-catching, clean, well lit? Are the windows clean?

Next, walk up to the front door of your office as if you had never seen it before. What is your first impression? Be honest with yourself – does it look classy and professional? Does it look warm and inviting? Does it make an impact on you or even make you say "Wow"? Walk in the front door and notice whether the carpets are clean or in good shape, whether the walls are nicely painted or wallpapered. Are all the lights inside the practice working; are the chairs and equipment clean and in good repair; are there beautiful pictures on the wall and are they hung straight; are the magazines in the reception area current, in good shape, and high quality.

Is there a warm smile and happy greeting from the receptionist when you walk in? Is she/he well groomed and professionally attired? Remember, the receptionist is your Department of First Impressions — through the telephone first and then when the patient arrives at the practice. This point can be a killer and can lose the practice income due to poor first contact.

**Now the fun part!**

Having done your inspection, the challenge is how to remedy any points that you may have found that need improving. Devise a battle plan for how you are going to attack these points. Prioritize them and systematically work down your list. If you don't have the funds for some, do the ones you can first.

**DON'T PROCRASTINATE. DO IT NOW!**

# NUMBER 25

## SMILE…

… and the whole world smiles with you!

Has anyone frowned at you lately? Did one of your friends or colleagues look a little serious or preoccupied? Did it make you feel good? Probably not!

There have been many studies to show that smiling increases your own personal health, but even further, if you smile at someone and it makes them smile back, then you have helped improve someone else's life and health.

In a healthcare practice, of course, you are all about the health of your patients. So keeping on smiling and finding things that are positive to smile about is going to make a difference.

It starts with the front desk setting the scene when a patient arrives. Big smile in greeting is the perfect thing to do. Technical staff – look serious, and you worry the patient or client. Doctor – same thing: getting a positive decision from them on their health care and as well as their on-going cooperation is much more likely if they are presented to with a smile.

Make it a practice policy to add more smiles to the daily agenda!

# NUMBER 26

## A Calm Environment

For your patients' sake as well as your own and your staff's, keeping a lid on tempers and angry outbursts in a practice is an important skill. Creating a calm working environment can increase the efficiency and level of production.

Getting angry may be the correct response to some situations. Yet blowing up and overreacting can ruin your relationships and success.

For example, you might feel outraged and say:

1. "WHO STOLE MY PEN?"
2. "I can't believe that you are late for work AGAIN!"
3. "How many times have I told you not to do it that way!"
4. "You try doing MY job and see how tough it is!"
5. "Why do you always jump to the conclusion that it is my fault whenever something goes wrong!"

Jumping to wrong conclusions and getting outraged can seriously damage your success.

### Know Before You Blow
Before you let anger take over as a reaction, ask questions to find out all the data and you might be surprised to find that there is no need to be upset at all.

1. "Has anyone seen my pen?"
2. "Why are you late?"
3. "Why did you do it that way?"
4. "What are you having trouble with?"
5. "What is the story here?"

The answers to these questions may open the door to finding the real situation and then allow for a correct solution to be implemented. CALMLY!

# NUMBER 27

## Show You Care

In the rush and crush of your daily practice, you may sometimes find yourself a little short on tenderness or empathy. Some of you seem to be born with more compassion than others.

Some may have to work on it and practice living in the other person's shoes to really get the hang of this. As a healthcare professional, you are working with people and need to be sensitive to making a positive experience for them.

### Suggestions:

Here are some tips and examples from some of our clients with respect to providing the caring, compassionate environment for the patients, clients and staff:

The 'waiting room' is referred to as the 'greeting room'. The whole idea is that patients/clients are there to be taken care of, not to wait.

When you are finished treating a patient, walk them out to the front and help them into their coat and shake their hand and tell them that it has been a pleasure to serve them. Many patients/clients will say, "No, it has been my pleasure."

Laugh, have fun, make the experience in your practice be a positive and pleasurable one. Focus on talking about positive things with the patients/clients rather than discussing bad news.

When a patient/client says, "I hate to complain…," say: "No, it is not a complaint — it is a concern."

Keep in mind that your practice is not all about making money; it is to deliver dedicated service. Work at that every day and you will do very well financially. Just put the emphasis on the service.

Create a pleasant environment of nice music, pictures on the walls, comfortable chairs, coffee, current magazines.

It's all about the patients/clients knowing that you care. Let them know that you do.

## Staff Are Important Too:

Notice that staff are very much included in the above statement. Stressed, unhappy staff don't deliver quality care. Creating a stress-free and cheerful working environment will not only attract patients but also good staff. Plus, it will help you keep them.

The staff can examine their own actions and interactions with patients/clients and compare themselves to the ideals set out in your mission statement. They can ask themselves when they mishandle something: Did that action provide the best quality care to our patients? Then they can work out how to do it better next time. Good staff are pretty self-correcting when they know what is expected of them.

# NUMBER 28

## The Face of Your Practice

When healthcare professionals say, "My front desk..." they are not usually referring to the piece of furniture in the reception area but rather to the living, breathing human being taking care of business at the front of the practice. This person is the "face" of your practice and hugely responsible for the success of your practice. And fortunately, most Receptionists definitely want the practice to be successful.

While it is a given that the position requires that the Receptionist knows how to type, file, greet, collect, schedule, talk to insurance companies, and use the computer (and chew gum all at the same time), there are more aspects to this job if one has an interest in the practice growing and reaching more people with the important services it offers.

For instance, the care and interest a Receptionist shows the patient or client when they arrive for their appointment and again when they are finished and departing, leave a patient or client with the feeling of goodwill toward the practice. Simply being polite and acknowledging the patient or client upon arrival is NOT the same as being greeted cheerfully and with a few kind words. Trust me, I am NOT saying to get into a long conversation because THAT is exactly what you don't want to do if you want to be efficient. It is a fine line to walk between the two extremes.

How about keeping the patient or client in contact with the practice between visits by creating a monthly email newsletter that goes out to every patient or client of record. This is way easier to do that most people know. There are templates on the internet and in Word that can be used where you just plop in little paragraphs of material that would be of interest to the patients/clients, but not a scientific diatribe; these can be gotten from non-competitor's websites, etc. There could be a monthly contest in it (best vacation picture of the month, cutest dog picture, best recipe of the month) wherein the winner is published the next month and is awarded a $100 gift certificate for Future Shop, or Tim Horton's, etc. This is just a fun feature that is not soliciting, nor breaking the Privacy Act, nor anything else – just a reason for the patient or client to look at your email each month and have some fun. It is a PR action.

How about doing a survey of patients or clients as to their favourite 3 magazines and when you have got 100 answers, then total them up and see which are the 5 most popular and buy those monthly for the waiting area.

Another PR action is for the Receptionist to go through all patient charts and find the ones that have not come in for more than two years and write them a heartfelt letter asking how they are doing and saying that everyone in the practice misses them.

Here's another one, and this could really be fun: Find a charity or a cause that everyone in the practice could participate in and get them involved. This is called "Social Responsibility" and is a way of contributing something to the world at large as a team. Of course, this activity can be captured in photographs and displayed on the bulletin board in the reception area. Patients or clients may even want to participate!

A practice is created by design. The living, breathing, caring person at the "front desk" is extremely important to the building of a successful practice!

Have fun with this and put some more "life" into the practice.

# NUMBER 29

## From Good to Great

Interested in increasing the flow of new patients or clients into your practice? If yes, you are not alone as about 95% of healthcare practices still have room to grow. Even if you are fully booked, there is always a need for new clientele because of natural attrition due to people moving on and passing on.

Since internal marketing is the least expensive way to find new business, the question is: How to inspire your patients or clients to actively refer to your practice? Referrals is obviously one of the best ways to acquire them, as the person being referred knows a bit about you and has heard enthusiastic things about you and your team. How to make this happen?

The answer is to take your practice from good to GREAT in terms of service delivered by you and your team. To start the process, do this exercise: Think of your favourite [high end, expensive] restaurant. What was the external appearance like? When you walked in, were you immediately greeted in a friendly and welcoming way that made you feel important? Did the Maître D' treat you graciously? Was your table immediately available and ready set? Did the waiter "make friends" (engage) with you and establish your expectancy for the evening? And so on. You get where I am going ... best possible performance from each and every staff member. And you have, as a result, probably referred other people to that restaurant for a delightful evening.

As you can see, this relates directly to your own practice. An extremely positive experience with no shocks, lots of education and understanding, and superlative care will impress anyone. No moods, no internal arguments, no ruffled feathers, no attitude. Just be GREAT! It is not only for the patient or client's sake ... you will all feel better just by doing this. You are on stage. Act GREAT!

Patients or clients in turn will be delighted to refer their friends and family to you. And then you will give them too the royal treatment and so you will grow.

And grow!

# NUMBER 30

## Taking Things Up a Notch

Have you noticed that people are expecting more and better service for their money than ever before? And have you ever sat down with your team and worked out in detail how each aspect of your practice could give a little more or better service to your patients or clients?

The practices or clinics that take service over the top are always the busiest ones and attract new patients easily through referrals.

There are many, many ways this extra service can be given. Believe it or not, how glad you or your staff sound when taking a phone call from a patient or client is noticed by them. When they walk in the front door of your practice, a wonderful smile and greeting from your front desk staff can make the patient or client feel very welcomed.

Of course, there are the follow up calls after a difficult treatment or service is always appreciated.

Running the practice on schedule impresses clients because you're showing your respect for them and that they are important.

Making notes in the computer or chart to ask the patient or client next time you see them how it went with the special event (graduation, christening, bar mitzvah, wedding, etc.) that they told you about the last time they were at the practice shows an interest in them.

Look for ways to deliver a better service than was expected or they feel they are paying for.

You get the concept, now have a meeting with the team and run with it. Your team will often surprise you with their creativeness.

# NUMBER 31

## Empathy: The HEART of the Practice

Ever worked with someone who, upon hearing a misfortune that you just experienced, reacted by saying, "You'll get over it, move on." Or, "Life sucks, nothing you can do about it." Or, "Really! You DO have a lot bad things happen to you, don't you?"

You could say that this person has "no heart." Clearly, they do not know the meaning of empathy! Basically, empathy has been described as the ability to relate to the thoughts, feelings and experiences of another person.

It does not mean sugary, syrupy sympathy which is rejected as "overdone" caring. Nor giving someone pity, also undesirable "care." Someone described empathy as "the ability to step into someone else's shoes and be aware of their feelings and needs." Let's add, "and let the person know that you have understood."

Whether you are dealing with a client, patient or a fellow member of your team, showing empathy requires that you really listen attentively to what the person is saying and put your complete focus on them. Put yourself in their shoes while you listen. If it is a patient or client, once you have completely understood their communication, you can then answer it or deal with it in a caring fashion.

With your staff or fellow team members, empathy shows a deep respect and care level. Sometimes all one needs is the feeling that someone has heard them, and then a really good strong acknowledgement to let them know they HAVE been heard. "Wow, I really GOT that." Once you have understood the whole picture, to be effective and helpful, you could then get the person to envision what they could do to handle the situation and focus them on being solution oriented, instead of being stuck in the problem.

Smooth, productive patient dealings and management of an office result from the empathy levels of the practice.

# NUMBER 32

## Client Loyalty – Stick in Their Minds

Client loyalty is a big issue these days with all the marketing that is thrown at them, such as Direct Mailing fliers from other practices. When your patients or clients are away from your practice, you are "out of sight, out of mind."

Therefore, building loyalty through more frequent contact or reminders of your practice can be beneficial. A cost effective and efficient way to keep your practice and services on their minds is through a monthly emailed newsletter.

For the more computer savvy who have a website and know how to make changes on it, also put your newsletter up there once a month and have your staff let all patients/clients know to look there for it. Most people have a computer or access to one nowadays.

**For the email newsletter, this is easy to do:**

1.  Build up an email address book in your computer by having your front desk staff start collecting email addresses from all your patients or clients. When your staff call patients for scheduling or confirming, coach them to ask for the person's email address as well and have them put it in the computer.

2.  Write a simple newsletter which could include the latest news that a patient or client should know, helpful tips, a cute joke, interesting tidbits, any successes, notifications of

changes of hours or office closure dates coming up, staff changes, etc. What would YOU like to read if YOU were receiving it? Photos speak a thousand words so be sure to include one or two of those. Keep them low resolution so your email isn't "heavy."

3. Send out a fresh newsletter each month. If you have a website, upload the newsletter there too.

Stay in people's minds and keep them loyal to your practice.

# NUMBER 33

## How to Increase Your Patient Referrals

One of the keys to a successful practice is having an abundance of new patients calling in and walking through your front door.

How do you do that without racking up a heavy advertising budget that could eat away all your hard-earned profits?

Oddly enough, the answer is right inside your practice! Namely, word of mouth from your already existing clientele.

Patients who are extremely happy and enthusiastic about the service they have received from you and your staff will readily refer family, friends, neighbors and co-workers, without much prodding or coaxing.

It is amazing how willing an enthusiastic patient is to have others experience the same level of care that they themselves have received.

In many instances, they will go out of their way to get someone else to come to you because your team delivers fantastic service and results.

Contrary to popular belief, satisfied patients do not refer. Patients enthusiastic about your service do refer.

To illustrate this point, here is an example:

Let's say that you are hungry, in a hurry and don't have much money in your pocket. You might run out to a burger joint, taco place or chicken hut – something very **fast**. In a short amount of time, you are no longer hungry and it didn't cost you an arm and a leg. So you could say that your criteria have all been met and you are satisfied, right?

Now let's take the opposite scenario. Let's say you go to your favorite upscale restaurant where it's very expensive, takes several hours to eat and, if you're like me, you eat it **all** because it is so delicious, and then you leave the restaurant with a bit of pain.

**Question:** If a friend asks you for the name of an excellent restaurant where they really take care of you and where he and his wife will have a great experience, which restaurant are you going to refer them to?

**Answer:** You most likely picked the second one. Why? Because you are enthusiastic about the ambience, top level service and care – even though it cost a lot, took longer and you hurt!

**Now ask yourself:** Do you want your practice to be like a fast-food restaurant **or** do you want to be a class act? If the answer is "a class act", remember this: When referrals are not coming in the door in sufficient quantity, focus on improving **service** and this in turn will increase the number of enthusiastic patients leaving your practice.

Here are some of the ways that it might be possible to improve the service and care levels in your practice:

Be sure to book your appointments in such a way that you can run on time. This is a courtesy point and impresses patients, even though they themselves sometimes run late.

Send a thank you card to any patient that refers someone to you. This reflects that you really appreciate their help and encourages further referrals.

Manners are an extremely key point in a healthcare practice or any other kind of business. From the front desk staff, to the dentist, the assistant and the hygienist. Patients respect those who treat them with respect and good manners.

Care about your patients. If you really don't care for them, you shouldn't be treating them. Find something about them that you like and focus on that. If you are short on caring, they will do the same to you, i.e. badmouth you or not pay their bill.

Give them the best quality dentistry for their money. Educate them so they want the best. When they have gone ahead with the ideal, they are much more likely to refer others to you.

Have a mission statement for the practice so that the staff and you are on the same page with regard to quality of care and service to the patients. Focus on it until it becomes habit.

After a major dental procedure, be sure to do a follow up call to ensure that all is well. Not all patients who are having difficulties will call you. This will show that you care about their well-being.

There are probably several thousand other ways to show you care. But there is no substitute for really caring.

When a patient is getting ready to leave the practice, do an "enthusiasm check". For instance, ask "Is there anything else that we can do to be of service to you today?" or "Is there anything we could have done better today – we're always looking for ways to evolve our practice to a higher level of care." The key point here is that the staff must be on the lookout to ensure that the patient is in fact enthusiastic about your service.

Fact: The patient who is enthusiastic about the service they received in your practice will bring in 2 to 8 new patients to you – at no charge! A patient who is only "satisfied", or worse yet, upset, will talk negatively about you to 10 to 12 people. Factually, they may keep coming back to you, but they won't refer other people to you.

So take these simple steps to increase your patient referrals:

1. Deliver excellent technical service

2. Make sure all staff care for the patient

3. Do an enthusiasm check as they leave

If the patient is not enthusiastic, find out what they are not happy with and work out how to remedy it.

And there you go. Simple but powerful steps which will lead to increased referrals, simply because you took the time and effort to improve your service level in all areas of the practice. So remember, when referrals are not coming in the door – focus on improving one area: service. Satisfied patients do not refer others to you, only enthusiastic patients refer.

# NUMBER 34

## How to Increase YOUR New Patient Numbers

No matter the number of years your practice has been in business, it is always healthy to have a steady flow of new patients coming into your practice in order to maintain a continual expansion.

Here is one way to increase the flow of new patients into your practice.

**Telephone Shopper Handling:**

**In many** practices, the front desk staff receives as many as 1 – 10 telephone shopper calls per week. While these calls can be a pain in the neck if the staff is very busy with patients coming and going and other administrative duties, these calls ARE very important to the growth of the practice.

Instead of thinking it's a call to get rid of, take it as an opportunity to get a new patient.

**Assume** the person calling needs your services and wants an appointment. Shoppers are not sitting at home dialing numbers to irritate you or your staff – they actually need and want something or they would not have called.

**Do not** try to rush through this call. Taking 5 minutes to build a rapport with the person will show that your practice believes in high quality care and attention to the patient. This will set your practice apart from others who merely "quote the fee" and ask "would you like an appointment". You should avoid making either of those errors.

If asked directly for fees right at the beginning of the call, say something like this: "I'll be happy to help you with that but first I need some information from you. What is the current difficulty you are experiencing? How did you hear about our practice?" Etc. Get answers.

**Then** tell the potential new patient: "It sounds like we should schedule you for an appointment as soon as possible. Is June 13th at 10 a.m. or 14th at 4 p.m. (give two options) better for you?" Find a time that works for them and get them scheduled. Get as much personal information filled in on your intake forms as possible "to save them the time" when they arrive for the first appointment. This firms up the commitment and is actually a nice service point.

**If they** again ask about costs, answer, "Our fees will vary depending on the treatment required. However, it can range between $_ to $_. We will not, however, start any treatment without your consent."

Use these tips and increase your new patients.

# PART 4:

# TIME MANAGEMENT

# NUMBER 35

## Procrastination! Are You Slowly Boiling to Death?

### First, the procrastination story:

There were these three researchers who took a baby frog and popped it into a pot of boiling water. What do you think the frog did? If you answered "jumped out," go to the head of the class! The impact was sudden enough to make it take quick, life-saving action.

Then they took the same frog and put it in a pot of cold water and slowly turned up the temperature until it reached boiling. In this case, what do you think the frog did? Of course, you guessed it: the answer is that he just slowly boiled to death. There was no moment of impact to make him jump.

### No Impact:

Running a practice on a daily basis can sometimes cause you to feel like you are slowly boiling to death. You keep putting off certain matters and decisions, until the heat of your stress reaches a slow boil.

In most practices, if you are paying attention to detail, there are many, many issues that should be addressed. Most of them are not big enough to hit you over the head (impact) and make you take immediate action. Instead, you procrastinate.

### Try this:

On each issue that you notice during the day that cannot be immediately handled, quickly make a note about it. Keep all the notes in one place. At the end of the day, before you walk out the door, sit down with your schedule and the sticky notes, and work out when you will take on each one and put it in your diary.

Then enter your reward that you give yourself at the end of your work week IF you did each of the actions you diarized for that week. No cheating either!

# NUMBER 36

## Beating Procrastination

Hewlett-Packard recently published the following tips on the internet and said to share it, so that is what we are doing. Enjoy!

Many of us juggle so many priorities that it's tempting to put things off until the last minute in our efforts to keep up with our work without losing our minds. However, procrastination can result in even more unnecessary stress if it happens too often – so here are a few ways to kick this bad habit.

### 1. Whenever possible, don't multi-task

When you're performing multiple tasks at once, it's easy to lose track of what you're doing and end up with tasks only partially completed. Try to focus on one task at a time until it is finished before moving on to the next – so you'll have no excuse for leaving something unfinished that you'll have to come back to later.

### 2. Set a timer

Many of us put off unpleasant tasks – it's simply human nature. To help make boring chores more palatable, tell yourself you'll only do the activity for a set amount of time – say ten or 15 minutes. After ten minutes, if you want to stop working, you can. Interestingly, if you give yourself permission to stop after ten minutes, you may find the momentum carries you along and you'll keep working anyway.

### 3. Reward yourself

Give yourself a bit of positive motivation to get things done. Tell yourself that once you've completed your task, you can go out to lunch with your colleagues. Or set up one-hour blocks of time where you focus entirely on work, followed by a fifteen-minute break with a favourite cup of tea. You might even think of the relief you'll feel once the task is completed – that's usually a reward in itself!

## 4. Make it as simple as you can

When starting a task that you've been putting off, the most important point is just to get started. Don't pay attention to the details right away, just focus on making a start. For example, if you need to prepare a report, just begin by writing down the most important points first. Don't worry about formatting it properly or finding the right words, just get it written down. This is a much less stressful and intimidating way to begin, especially for larger, complex projects.

While procrastination may be difficult to overcome, the strategies above can help you keep yourself on track. And don't forget to be kind to yourself – hard work deserves "downtime", so be sure you're not working so hard that you're burning out. Coming to work refreshed and rested can be the best preventative measure against procrastination.

# NUMBER 37

## The Do-It-Now Habit

Do you feel overworked? Do you have too much to do? Are you not making the progress you want to be making toward your goals?

Why can some people produce twice as much as others? Some people are SO efficient and organized they can make you feel like you are standing still.

For example, Jane not only handles three kids, but works 30 hours per week and runs a small business from her home office. Her house is always clean and she prepares delicious, healthy meals for her family.

Jill, on the other hand, has one daughter, makes no money, has no time to do her housework and prefers pizza delivery dinners.

To be more like Jane and less like Jill, break the bad habits and form a new good habit.

### What is the Bad Habit?

The bad habit is seeing something you need to do – a task, a program, a phone message, an assignment, walk the dog, etc. – and deciding to do it later.

Instead of DOING it now, you look at it, think about doing it, consider the problems, sigh, and leave it for "later". Nothing is accomplished. A total waste of time.

### Form the Do-It-Now Habit

When you jump and do things at your first opportunity, you stay in better control of your job and your life while earning hours of extra time to use however you wish.

The best time to get into a do-it-now habit is, of course, RIGHT NOW!

1. Take a stack of papers, task or any kind of cluttered mess that you need to handle.

2. Take the first item.

3. Deal with it, handle it, do it now.

4. If you find it hard to do it now, make a reward. By increasing your efficiency, you will have "spare" time to use how you wish.

# NUMBER 38

## Next Level = More STRESS?

Many healthcare professionals whom we have had the pleasure of working with equated the idea of expanding their practice with doubling the current stress.

But does it have to be? In a word, "**NO!**"

*Here are a couple of Quick Tips to help you improve the current scene and then to expand smoothly without adding stress:*

Start at the top – that's you! Are you fully utilizing your technical team to the max? To increase your efficiency, work out what you are doing that could legally be done by your staff. Turn over these functions.

Adjust your practice hours to suit your life. Stress comes in different shapes and sizes, and an odd one is getting stressed out when your day runs overtime and you have to pick up the kids after school, etc. In that case, starting the day a little earlier and ending a little sooner could completely reduce your stress.

Work out with your receptionist how you would like her to book your "Ideal Day" for the least amount of stress for you. Let her know what kind of work you want to do and when and where in your schedule.

Staff accountability – you should have specific functions being done by specific individuals so that they are accountable for those activities. It streamlines your management, because you now have an exact individual to go to if something isn't working well, and also if it is working **VERY** well and you want to capture that and keep it going.

Improve internal marketing. Work out ways to improve quality of care and service to your patients. Think like a patient and go through the practice looking at ways to increase the quality of patient care.

# NUMBER 39

## Organize for Success

Success seems to come to some people more easily than others. What are the secrets to achieving those dreams we dream? How can we make it easier and faster to reach those dreams?

One of the answers is: **ORGANIZATION**.

If you observe highly productive people who are getting a lot done and are achieving their goals, you will notice that they are usually very well organized.

They get the most possible productivity with the least amount of time and effort. Their work space is orderly and clean. Their possessions are kept in good working order and easy to locate. They are punctual, dependable and efficient.

Organized people stay on top of the routine actions necessary to successful living. Their cars run well, their desks are clean and their files are orderly. They set goals, work out doable plans and figure out their priorities. Because they are organized and ready to produce, they get more things done than people who are disorganized.

You, too, must be organized in order to achieve your dreams. You could start the process by looking closely at the current state of organization at your practice, of your employees, of your home, etc. Note which areas could be more organized and what specifically needs organizing. Then make a plan of attack for each area and do one area at a time until done.

**Suggestion:**

Start with the simplest one first. Then the next simplest.

When you have raised the level of organization in your life, you will perform better, accomplish more and make your dreams into reality!

# NUMBER 40

## Scheduling "The Ideal Day"

If you want happier staff, if you want to run on time and if you want more enthusiastic patients, consider scheduling "Ideal Days." An Ideal Day must first be defined and then all appointments scheduled in accordance to this definition.

When defining an ideal day there are a number of factors which must be considered. All practitioners are not the same, nor do they like to practice in the same manner or at the same speed.

Nonetheless, there is an ideal day for each one.

One way to start the process is to work out the revenue you want to generate that day and your preferences re types of appointments or patients that you want to see. The revenue aspect can be calculated fairly easily. How much money do you want to make divided by the number of days that you plan to work? The result is a per day amount.

Can you produce this amount on a consistent daily basis?

Can you arrange your appointments so you can produce this amount?

What must the appointment book look like in order to produce this (how many long appointments versus how many short appointments)?

**You must define the optimum schedule and then show your staff how to book you accordingly.**

In terms of patient types, you will have preferences in how they are to be scheduled as well. For example, patients who require additional or special care can be very trying on a practitioner if not scheduled correctly. This can be avoided by issuing explicit instructions to your staff about what you don't want to appear in your book and, of course, ensuring that they are carried through with.

No matter which of the above are being phased in, they have to be monitored and often retuned until you get exactly the result you want. Whether you get what you want or not is often a question of how persistent you are in terms of carrying through on your ideal day protocols. Monitor your appointment book and continue to groove in the new procedures for the way you want to be booked.

# NUMBER 41

## Time Management Tips

### BUSY, FRUSTRATED AND/OR STRESSED?

Have you ever been "busy" all day, but didn't achieve your goals?

You were probably distracted. Ever wonder why you feel frustrated at work? Distractions might be stopping you. Ever feel stressed? Distractions may be slowing you down.

Distractions are not just irritating; they are destructive forces that ruin your productivity.

Examples:

- supplies that ran out unexpectedly

- salespeople who drop in without appointments

- discussions about personal problems

- sunny days,

- rainy days

- holidays

- gas prices

- diets

- money

- health problems

- and more!

How do you handle distractions?

Get organized.

A well-organized business understands distractions and organizes to deal with them. For instance, a morning meeting to plan the day with your staff can take up the admin issues that need to be dealt with; someone delegated to be in charge of supplies and a system of written notification of supplies that are getting low BEFORE they run out and it becomes an emergency; a policy that personal phone calls are to be dealt with OFF of production time, etc.

**Time Management Strategy:**

For a few days, note down on a pad every distraction that happens. Then sit down with your staff in a meeting and work out what systems and policies will handle those. Everyone had a hand in creating the systems, so there is more ownership of the policies and they will be adhered to better.

You make much faster progress toward your goals and ultimate success when you are well-organized and not distracted.

# NUMBER 42

## Are You a Top Performer?

To explain their failures, you might hear people say:

- *"I don't have a head for business which is why my practice is not doing well."*
- *"Leaders are born to lead. I was born to follow. I'll just be a good soldier."*
- *"She inherited her musical skill from her father, but my dad is a truck driver which is why I can't play the piano."*

If you believe you need to inherit a skill or a talent to be successful, you are one step closer to failure. If you realize you can get the talent to succeed at anything you wish, you are one step closer to success. So if talent is not something you are born with, where do you get it?

How did Michael Jordan become the greatest basketball player of all time? What made Luciano Pavarotti into a great opera singer? Why was Warren Buffet such a brilliant investor?

Are these professionals born with their skills? Actually, no. The most successful people achieved their greatness through hard, intense training and practice.

**Practice, practice, practice. Hours and hours of practice.**

For instance, Winston Churchill, one of the world's greatest speakers, practiced his speeches compulsively. Michael Jordan was cut from his high school team which proves his talent was not "natural." Instead, he practiced his famous basketball moves for more hours every day than anyone else in the game.

For example, hitting a bucket of gold balls for fun is not practice, which is why most golfers don't improve. Practice means you hit 300 balls with the same club, with the goal of leaving the ball within 20 feet of the same spot. And you do this every day.

For an artist, practice means you paint the same flower 300 times until people gasp with pleasure when they look at it.

To succeed as a manager, you need to spend many hours bringing out the best performance possible from each of your employees. Role-playing and practicing will bring success.

Every skill can be practised and improved: handling shoppers on the phone, doing a technical procedure, using computers, managing money…everything.

The intention to improve and the constant practice will bring about the skill and "talent" you need to succeed.

# NUMBER 43

## Winging It

The other day as I was analyzing a practice, I asked the doctor if she manages by statistics and she replied, "No, we wing it." She had the grace to laugh as she said it, knowing that that was a less than optimum answer for her practice.

Ever wondered why your practice stats go up and down for no known reason? Have your annual profits stopped growing? Did you know that most practices lose substantial amounts of potential income on a weekly, monthly and annual basis due to insufficient attention to statistical management?

For example, Dr. Jones's billings jumped up steeply this week and he doesn't notice it because he doesn't analyze his weekly stats and take the appropriate actions the following week to cause them to improve. As a result, he fails to find out that a really good marketing change was made without his even being aware of it. If he had investigated, he would have found out that he also had 12 New Patients this week (instead of the usual 5) which in turn bumped up the overall billings.

In further looking into this, he would have asked the receptionist for any info she had on the huge increase in NP's. He would have been pleasantly surprised to find out that she started asking existing patients if they had any friends, family, neighbours or co-workers that they wanted to refer to the practice; and the extra 7 NP's this week were all referrals from the patients she had asked. In further questioning, he would have found out that she started asking for referrals after she read a practice management article on how to do it and she tried it out.

Voila, he now has the real reason for the sudden growth. Now, to keep it up in the same range or growing even further, he would need to encourage the receptionist to keep on doing this. A commendation in front of the team for her might go a long way, or a simple bonus, etc.

This is called management by statistics. Managing by emotions, guesswork and other systems is just poor management and can be quite frustrating and often results in overwork and less profitability.

# NUMBER 44

## Increase Your Survival Potential

Knowing how a practice is performing and how to increase its profitability are most efficiently accomplished through the use of statistics. Some people call them "performance metrics" and others may say "practice metric monitors," but in any case, they are referring to the numbers which measure the productivity of the various areas of the practice.

Statistics are like car gauges. They tell you whether something is wrong or right, as the case may be. Oil and water pressures in the expected range on the gauges mean things are normal. When an engine light comes on, you know you need to go to a service station to take care of it.

In your practice, statistics in the practice should have the same effect. They are objective measures and if you know how to read them on properly scaled graphs, they will guide you in what actions you need to take for increased expansion and profitability.

**Sample statistics to keep:**

- Number of New Patients for the week
- Weekly and Monthly Billing
- Weekly and Monthly Collections
- Average Daily Production (Monthly Billings Divided by Number of Days Worked)
- Weekly Billings by Provider
- Overhead (Expenses)
- And so on

[114]

"Monitoring" or "watching" stats is NOT statistical management – it is being a spectator. An executive takes appropriate actions based on the weekly and monthly statistical results.

The skill in managing by statistics is finding out what changed, up or down and fixing it. Part of this process is having sufficient statistics so you can isolate the exact problem area or, on the positive side, the area that is causing the overall statistics to be up.

**So MAKE your survival potential go UP by MANAGING by statistics!**

# NUMBER 45

## Does One or More of the Following Ring True for You?

- Though hardworking, you're frustrated at your lack of progress.

- Your New Year's resolutions are the same year after year.

- You're discouraged by the many things you're NOT getting done.

- You're dissatisfied with the unimportant things you ARE getting done.

Being the CEO of a practice is not always easy, especially considering that an overriding amount of your time is spent being the healthcare provider as well as a dizzying number of other functions.

Being as this is the start of a New Year, why don't you give yourself a treat and put aside some time to set your goals for this year – personal and practice-related. There is a saying, "You can't get THERE if you don't know where THERE is." Perhaps writing down (in detail) where you want to arrive at will get you excited about making some changes.

Here's an example of what happens when you DON'T do proper planning: Many practitioners sit down at the end of the month and without any planning in place, simply write out cheques for all their creditors, and then pay themselves the balance of what is in the bank account.

They fail to allocate a monthly budgeted amount for marketing or promotion in order to drive in more business which would ultimately result in more income for the practice. No planning! No growth!

If you are interested in learning how to be the CEO of your practice and make this year be the best ever year, call us and meet with one of our Strategists!

# NUMBER 46

## It's Not Too Late...

...to make your New Year Resolutions stick!

### 1. Powerful Goals

When making or setting your goals, THINK BIG, but don't go outside of your concept of reality. Be very specific ... in fact, the more specific you are, the more chance you have of accomplishing them. They may be short term or long term. If the goal is very large, break it down to smaller sub goals so you achieve success.

### 2. Action Plan

Now you need to break down the overall goal into a doable, step by step plan of attack. Make sure the steps are small enough to encourage rapid completion and thus create a strong sense of achievement.

### 3. Tick the Boxes

Once a week at a specified time have a meeting with yourself (and anyone helping you) and tick off the items that have been completed. Determine which ones you are going to accomplish in the next week.

### 4. Back on Track

If you fall off the wagon and miss a week, just get yourself back on track and CONTINUE! Do not let any momentary halts or slip-ups bring you to a full stop. Just pick up where you left off and continue.

### 5. Reward Thyself (and anyone who helped you).

Don't forget that rewards for meeting goals, big or small, create a positive experience by putting pleasure into the picture. Smaller rewards for meeting smaller goals, and a WHOPPER for achieving the final goal.

[118]

# NUMBER 47

## How Do You Handle Life's Roadblocks?

When you feel stopped from accomplishing something, how do you respond? Get frustrated and give up? Drown your sorrows? Blame others? Blame yourself? Finding excuses is a popular way of explaining why you didn't meet your goal. And of course, many people just give up.

But how SHOULD you handle life's roadblocks?

Write down your top three goals. If you don't have three top goals, write down three big things you really want.

Put these goals where you will see them several times each day. For example, a note taped on your car's dashboard ... a note on your computer screen ... put it in your scheduler in your phone in a way that it will come up every day ... place a sticker on the inside of your wallet. Anywhere you will constantly see the goals.

Every time you feel like it can't be done or a roadblock appears, refuse to get sad or give up or look for excuses. Instead, look over your goals again and renew your interest in achieving them. Become solution-oriented instead of buying into "why it can't be done."

If you constantly have in mind where you are going, and you persist, YOU WILL GET THERE! You will need to work at it consistently. You will usually find that it takes time and energy to reach those goals.

**Keep focused and strong intentioned and there is no obstacle that will be big enough or strong enough to stop you!**

# PART 5:

# SUCCESS

# Number 48

## Making Success

Many people in this world are spectators, watching the world news and the good and bad things happening around them, but not working out solutions or the handlings needed. They are waiting for something to happen. They are followers, not leaders, and so find themselves at the receiving end of a lot of undesirable effects. Throwing up their hands and saying that nothing can be done about it is apathy and is a very unsatisfactory way of life.

### Create the Goals First:

To make yourself successful, you must start with making strong goals that you want to achieve more than anything else. It can be for yourself personally, and for your family, and another for your business, and maybe even some kind of contribution that helps mankind as a whole.

The future is like an empty field. No one is playing on it yet. You can run out there and start the game.

### Get Agreement and Willingness to Help:

You need to really WANT to reach these goals and put passion into them and get everyone connected with the goals to be in agreement and wanting to help achieve them. Many goals take a whole group to bring about and there needs to be really cool rewards for reaching very stiff goals.

### Take the First Step:

Sit down and take one goal at a time and work out the steps in sequence that you need to take to bring it about. When you are happy with that, set a time frame for it to be accomplished in. Then, TAKE THE FIRST STEP and get it done. Then the next, and so on.

**Keep it Fresh:**

Some people post these goals and steps on their fridge, or on their bulletin board at the office if it is for the practice. This keeps it in their face and fresh. They then mark off each step as it is accomplished. Finally, when the last step is done, THEY CELEBRATE!

And here is the most important thing at this point: MAKE A NEW GOAL and get going on THAT one.

# NUMBER 49

## Success Happens

Some people think success is only for the "lucky" or that "it's a matter of being in the right place at the right time" or that "it's who you know."

While it is a fact that there are people who have succeeded due to the above factors, did you know that **everyone** else can have success too?

Many healthcare professionals have told me over the last 25 years that the reason their stats in the practice are down is because …there's a recession happening … the weather was really bad this year … the whole town is going downhill … there are no good staff to be found to help out … and so on.

These are all "reasons" and do not allow for a solution. We have found routinely that a practice will grow very substantially, no matter the external circumstances, **if it is well run inside**. During the early 1990's when we had a major recession, our clients' practices grew a minimum of $10,000 per month routinely.

Voila! Your success actually depends on your ability to **deliver** a service or an object or task that others want. They pay you for this production so you can buy food, shelter and so on. Let's call this service, object or task your "product".

The more **valuable** your product the more money you earn. The more efficiently you produce your product, the more money you earn. The better manager you are of your staff and your time, the more money you earn. The more you know about marketing and actually do it, the more income you will earn. The higher the perceived quality of your service, the more you will earn.

Have a look at these factors in your practice or your job, and see what can be improved. Your income will follow that improvement.

# NUMBER 50

## Making it Happen

Over the years I have seen some of the most brilliant ideas fail. The reason being that the planning to get the idea implemented was poor, incomplete or non-existent. Any idea or change should be planned out to ensure that it gets fully carried out.

Once you have the idea or change, you must sit back and then work out in detail exactly what you are going to do to get it implemented step by step and in what sequence. It is a management role to plan and to make that planning become an actuality. Don't expect your staff to understand all the ramifications of your brilliant idea without a detailed explanation and a step by step plan of how to get everything done.

You must determine who is going to oversee the project (it doesn't have to be you), what is the purpose of getting this done, who is going to be doing what steps of the implementation and what resources are available, do I have the necessary expertise in-house or do I have to go outside, etc.

Lay it all out step by step and assign each step to someone. Without the assignment of steps to specific individuals you will end up doing it all yourself.

The last action is following up and making sure that the targets are being completed and completed in a timely fashion. Without management follow up great ideas often get bogged down and go nowhere. Be prepared to work with the individuals assigned specific targets and help sort things out so they can actually get the target done. Do not do the target yourself but rather get the individual more able to do it themselves. This will give you an even better resource for the next project you tackle.

Typically changes and new ideas are viewed by staff as additional work and so you must get them to see the advantages to themselves, the practice and the patients. Most staff are willing but they do need to be kept informed.

Getting ahead is a lot easier if you have an exact plan!

# NUMBER 51

## Imagine A Better Future

When you are hit with all the bad news of the world through radio, newspaper, friends, internet, and/or TV, it is sometimes hard to see a better future. Also, sometimes you have an idea that you want to achieve but never seem to get around to doing it and you feel sad that you have never fulfilled that dream.

Well, there IS something very interesting that you CAN do about all that: Use your imagination!

I learned a great tool from a friend the other day: To create a better future or take control of it more successfully, write down an area of your life that you would like to have go in a better direction, or a goal you would like to accomplish. This could be your practice, your family, your house, a hobby, a sports activity, etc.

Then use your imagination to visualize how you would like that aspect of your life to be. Really take some time to write down as much detail as you can about how you would like it be in an ideal world. Be as creative and as specific as you can. Think big. Don't let any negativity creep in or other people's opinions.

Example for a healthcare professional:

I want a big practice where I help a lot of patients. I want a team to work with me who come into work everyday on time and enthusiastic about the day ahead, and who get things done on their own initiative without very much supervision. I want a staff who are imaginative and creative and come up with new ways to grow the practice. I would like them to give perfect service to every patient or client. I want them to leave personal problems outside the practice. I would like them, when needed, to offer to stay late without my begging them to. I wish to have patients/clients who want to go ahead with ideal care that I present to them. I would like perfect days where everyone shows up for their appointments on time. Being paid promptly and in full would be great. I want to buy my own building to move the practice into on a busy street with our own parking lot. (And so on… you get the idea.)

Then write out each point in a list. Put that in a place where you see it every day and use that excellent imagination of yours to start working out, bit by bit, how you can make each point become a reality.

# NUMBER 52

## The Power of Intention

Have you ever thought to yourself, "I should get up and get this ____ done?" And it didn't happen. Or have you seen someone give a weak order, "You should move those files someday." And it didn't get done.

One skill that great leaders have that puts them in control of situations is the strength of their intention to get something done or make something happen. You have to direct your mind to the result that you want and put that across to the other person. When you use the correct level of intention in your communication, people pay attention to you and you get better results.

For example, if you tell your children to clean up their rooms with weak intention, they continue to play around. If you tell them with strong intention, it gets done.

### Intention at Work:

Your job is easier when you use the correct amount of intention to make something happen. For example, a co-worker named Chris likes to complain to you. Chris says, "I hate this crappy chair." "This weather is horrible." "Oh no, here comes Mr. Big again."

Tolerating or avoiding Chris resolves nothing. Your workplace remains stressful. Yet if you look Chris in the eye and say, "Chris, stop complaining," using full intention for that happen, you will enjoy some wonderful results.

A manager with poor intention gets little cooperation and eventually fails. However, a manager with strong intention finds that his or her employees usually do what they were hired to do.

Practice this until you become good at it. And get more done!

# NUMBER 53

## Vision for your Practice

Internal marketing has hundreds of aspects to it, but there are some that are more vital than others. Having a "vision" for the practice is one of these.

While more money may be an underlying motivation for growing your practice, you won't find many patients or clients that want to come into your practice to give you their hard earned money to make you rich. And staff definitely don't come to work every day to make the owner rich. That is NOT their vision.

Creating a Vision that everyone can agree with requires that it be inspiring to you (first and foremost), to your staff, to your patients/clients and to potential patients or clients.

Here are some samples from outside the healthcare world but these will give you ideas of how you could word yours:

Disney: Using our imagination to make people happy.

Whole Foods: Changing the way the world eats.

Southwest Airlines: To give people the freedom to fly. (have cheap airfares)

BMW: Giving people the joy of driving.

Walmart: Save money. Live better.

Apparently, those companies' that operate with a strong Purpose or Vision are 6 times more profitable than their competitors. This would be true for healthcare practices as well.

The Vision can be used to make your staff prouder of where they work when they see it in action every day. Let's say yours is: "To give the people of (your town/city) something to smile about." You could then make a goal to have 5% of your town's population as your patients or clients. Then do a marketing campaign around that which would include more and better service internally too. Patients or clients can be gotten on board to play the game by telling their friends and family about you, "liking" things on your Facebook, blogging about you and your team, etc.

Have a staff meeting and play around with this and see what comes out of it for starters. Be inspiring.

# NUMBER 54

## Is it FACTUALLY Possible to PRACTICE with PLEASURE?

Are you a frustrated practice owner? Are you stressed out? Are there days you feel like quitting?

YOU ARE NOT ALONE! Here are a bunch of statements made by practice owners BEFORE they hired us. Do any ring true for you?

"I was working hard, but seemed to be progressing only very slowly."

"I knew nothing and had no interest in the area of management."

"The addition of a new associate had stalled my patient flow."

"I soon became overwhelmed with the responsibility of managing."

"A year ago, I was ready to quit dentistry. Every day seemed dull and uninteresting."

"Life was hectic and stressful!"

"I was having a hard time managing my two offices."

"Tired and overwhelmed by the daily grind and demands in my life …"

"I always had steady growth but also ever increasing stress levels."

## HERE ARE THE OUTCOMES AFTER HELP FROM AMI:

"It helps you embellish YOUR vision of YOUR practice. No cookie cutter solutions here! You are in the driver's seat and you can take your practice anywhere you want."

"I have surpassed my expectations and I am thrilled…"

"AMI helped our practice to be more efficient, productive, organized, and helped us to be able to run the office as managers."

"The financial return has been quite significant as well."

"The end result is I am much happier and our overall office environment is much more enjoyable. ... happy, content staff."

"Now I have more time at home with my family and more free time for activities outside the office."

"AMI taught me to plan with success in mind and move ahead and take charge."

"More than this being an investment into my practice, it has been an investment into a better life."

"It has empowered me to take control of my practice and achieve a level of productivity I never thought possible one year ago."

"After almost 20 years in practice, I never imagined that work could still be so much fun and exciting."

"My practice has doubled in production since taking the course."

"They [AMI] trained me as the owner to be a better manager and a smarter business person."

# NUMBER 55

## What Works When Managing Your Practice?

Which of these five statements do you believe are true?

*"My business rises and falls based on the economy."*

*"My success is largely determined by luck."*

*"The weather influences my numbers hugely."*

*"I believe in fate and whatever happens, happens."*

*"My income controls me more than I control it."*

Of course, all of these statements are false. **YOU** are the one who **CONTROLS** your success.

One way to control your pay and your future is with statistics. We have noticed in consulting over 1,500 healthcare professionals that those who track and USE their statistics to make positive changes, take home more pay and have less stress. These should be kept on graphs for a visual look at your progress towards your goals.

When we say "statistics," here are a few examples: billings, collections, number of new patients or clients, expenses, marketing, and so on. Every valuable activity can be represented by a number. These stats should be tabulated and evaluated on a weekly basis. Daily can be a bit microscopic, whereas a month is a bit too late.

When a stat is down for the week, you want to immediately investigate WHY and handle the situation so it does not repeat, EVER.

Similarly, when a stat goes up for the week, you want to immediately investigate to find the actual reason and then repeat whatever successful action was isolated. Be sure to really look closely and find the REAL reason, not someone's "guess."

You can't "take control" of a practice without finding out what works and what doesn't. When it is under control, you can then have such things as bonus systems.

Try it, you just might like feeling more in control and less stressed!

# NUMBER 56

## Breaking Through Your Glass Ceiling

### Complacency and apathy:

Complacency is probably the number one enemy of practitioners in all professions. Trapped in a daily pattern of delivery and thinking that nothing can change is an apathy that slowly sneaks up on many healthcare providers. Some even think that they are doing the best that can be done, yet they have no yardstick to judge how much more and better quality service they actually COULD be delivering. They have hit their personal glass ceiling.

### Practice analysis:

Having analyzed over 5,000 practices one by one over the past 27 years, I have met many a practice owner who met with me in the hope that I could discover what was the matter with their practice and how to take them beyond their glass ceiling and make the practice grow some more (without killing them at the same time through long hours, more stress, etc.).

### Statistics are flat or going down:

However, some met with me to convince me that they are already doing everything that can be done. Their minds were closed. Some did not even know that they are billing only ½ to ¾ of what they should or could be. A few had gone into agreement with practitioner friends who were doing poorly and blamed it on the recession (there isn't one in Canada that we have found – statistics and production are caused inside the practice, not outside) and no longer sought to find out the REAL reason their stats were down or low. Very dangerous "friends."

### Practice stagnating; frustrated; overwhelmed:

Others had grown complacent with their staff and so the staff too was stagnating and no longer trying out new ideas. Many owners felt frustrated that they had not been taught management skills in college. Some had gotten overwhelmed by financial responsibilities in their lives and practices, and were ready to give up.

**Adventurous, aspiring, achieving:**

Then there were those who met with me to seek new tools and new creativity, to achieve fresh thinking, to demand knowledge. They were curious to learn and wanting more adventure. And it is with pleasure that we have helped them achieve those goals and kept them aspiring to be better – for the sake of their patients, their staff, themselves and their families.

I have for a long time subscribed to the belief that joy and happiness comes from constantly seeking and discovering new and better ways to do things, and going ahead to achieve my goals against any and all odds.

Here are three great quotes to take to heart:

*The arrogance of success is to think that what we did yesterday is good enough for tomorrow. – William Pollard*

*To think creatively, we must be able to look afresh at what we normally take for granted. – George Keller*

*Routine and predictable days are the breeding grounds for complacency. – Wayne Goodall*

Janice Wheeler is the President and co-owner of The Art Of Management Inc. (AMI), Canada's largest practice management company.

Since 1989, AMI has worked one on one with practice owners, training them to be better leaders in their practice, and giving them the ability to have the lives they have always dreamed of, whether in the practice or outside.

# WANT MORE?

Contact The Art Of Management Inc., and find out how to join the cast of healthcare professionals that are enjoying successful practices, spending more time with their families, and living the lives they could only dream of before learning the art of managing their practices.

The Art Of Management Inc.
200 Ronson Drive, Suite 203
Toronto, Ontario M9W 5Z9
1-800-563-3994

Made in the USA
Middletown, DE
05 February 2017